Yesterday

Nadia Brady

Presentation by *BookLeaf Publishing*

Web: www.bookleafpub.com

E-mail: info@bookleafpub.com

ISBN: 9789357446754

First edition 2022

This anthology is dedicated to the people their
loved ones left behind.

ACKNOWLEDGEMENT

My gratitude, eternally, to the ones who have
nourished the poet within me.

PREFACE

Poet. Writer. Daughter. Sister. Wife. Friend. I am often a wanderer, sometimes a warrior, always a seeker of truth and beauty in all its forms.

Elegy

Demeter,
You shielded me from stars,
and laid me in your molten womb.
I only died a little.

Charon,
brandishing headlights,
you drove your Honda
to cater Death's company,
thinking Death only worked days,
after all.

Aphrodite,
Glowing with your garnet ring,
you told me to sing
how grace had saved a wretch like me,
but you were the goddess of love,
not grace.

Atlas,
You carried me on your shoulders,
but the weight of the world was there, too.
A Titan can only hold so much
Before the earth begins to quake.

Eris,
Can't you handle the chaos you create?
The apple you threw

carries our bruises.

Morpheus,
I am done arguing with your dreams.
They are as real as your promise
to see my children.

Eurydice,
I should have known you would take me with you.

2

Foster

I have been trying so hard to save you,
thinking I could hold you together
with my charred wings.
I sing into your darkness,
and hold my breath.
I am waiting to blow the ashes from your eyes,
but you are right,
I am wrong,
and you won't open your eyes anyway.

The Island

He drank the kisses of a girl named
Salt and woke up with sand in his hair.
A diver in turquoise curls, he searched
for secrets her whim might whisper.
Every pearl caught,
filtered through their fingers
foam and sand.

Poetry

the words are lumps in our throats
we cannot swallow
the voice that sings to us
stripped naked and raw

Snow

you know I could kiss
every one of your fingers
but did you know
I know your nose and teeth
every noise
as you sink
into an ocean bed of sleep
the gentle outs past rosebud lips
the way your sleepy tongue begins to lisp
and the blustering ins
because you know
there is more than one meaning to the word snow
you are breathing in darkness with light lungs
nicotine is stealing your dreams
I am watching them dissolve
I wish I knew the you who dreamed
lucent
and raw
like the crystal lines
you cut with cards
our winter house of cards
is shaking
summer is coming
our foundation
almost
showing

Curiosity

I must know what happens.
It's my worst trouble.
I could be swept into nothingness
and look around.

Two Sisters

I found two freckles on my left shoulder,
the sweatshirt my sister outgrew covers seven more.
I can't remember how long I have had these gifts.
The sun doesn't remember either,
when the moon took note,
wrote The Seven Sisters for my shoulder as she
paused pulling the tides
the Tuesday I was born.
I was born asking for stories,
and the sun answers my skin
with a tale twenty years ago,
the story sisters have outgrown.

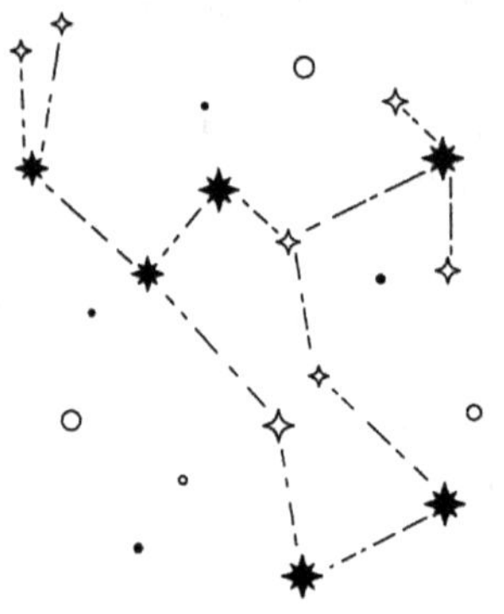

Lineage

My father,
your body is swallowing you whole.
I have searched like
we are starving
for the parts that you need,
but I am tired
of my own hungry fear.
It wells at my throat
after gutting me,
and now it wants my voice.
Like my mother,
I have found myself empty,
but I will give every part
that is left.

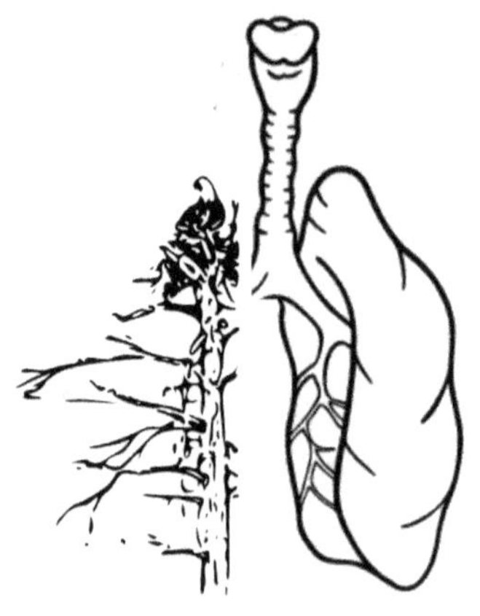

Yesterday Daughter

Come and see your yesterday daughter.
She is wearing your sundress like a cape.
Your pearl necklace is her tiara,
caught on her nose, she knows
she is cross eyed, and that you are about to
laugh or cry. You haven't decided which,
because your yesterday daughter will be here
tomorrow, but you will be her yesterday
mother. Setting with the sun,
you will be gone by tomorrow.

Inheritance

I'm not sure
forgive or not
forgive me
my mother should have told me
people are flawed
be lenient
have courage
in her silence
she told me
never forget

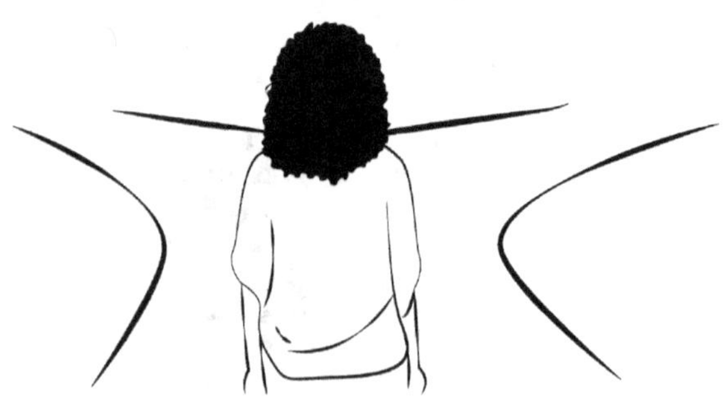

Mother

In the spring she remembers
the chamomile they planted
in the willow tree's shadow
more than twenty summers ago.
It was the wrong time for planting
and the seeds they buried
bore no fruit.

In the Garden

Behind the house slept garden stones, moss kissed
by the moon and rain. Its path arranged across
the yard for the forest line and the broken bush.
A spider crafting cornered clouds had breathed
the lie for flies to offer themselves blind
and warm for pale new nymphs of silken hunt.
The flies would give their young to her, naïve
to siren's song, and answer widow's call.

Why

You keep the anger for yourself, bitter
and stale under your tongue, saved
from a different fight.
The sky spits at the windshield,
and the street lamps, blinking
to the rain, ask you to slow
down the white grip, teeth
pressed, foot to the road.
When the sedan stops, you don't
know until the lights of the rubberneckers
are on you, asking why.

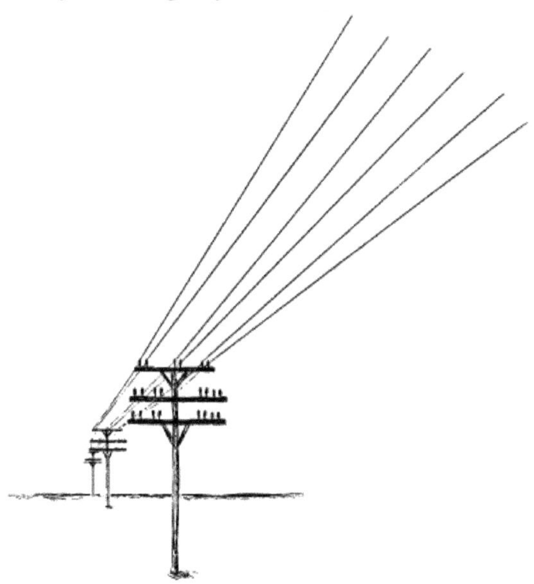

Lost House

No caps and coats collecting in my closets
or tread and tracks on tired mudroom floors.
Not like my drawn drapes can cite
when the clock last struck and shook the dust,
or rings and knocks have rallied runners to the door.
Not like the sun smiling on stained carpets
or plans for Saturday. No flushed retreats
from chasing winds that bit at apple cheeks.
Not like bones creaking, climbed at midnight,
now forgotten - the home I used to be.

Memère

My mother's favorite bedtime story to tell
was that when I was a baby, my grandparents
would time their visits so efficiently
that I never spent a moment with them.
Cribbed and mute on my blanket corner
she taught me to never see
anyone but her.
After my mother began hopping hospital
beds, jerry chairs, ICU to hospice,
I noticed the cancer in her collection of stories.
The night of the funeral,
siblings, cousins, and aunts filled
every bed and couch, but my grandmother
was awake, holding her loss, unraveling
yarn, clouds in her hands.
I sat down on the empty side of the quilted bed,
telling her a bedtime story tucked
in with a question. She answered,
hurricane arms pulling me into its eye
with all of the kindness my mother
never had, and told me a story.

The Seeded Truth

Daughter, you need to understand the dangers of a
seed, unheeded.

You should know that a seed will drink you, and your
body is a spring.
You should know that you are ripe, and it will leave
you, hollow
and jaundiced, roots aging,
vines amber.

You will want the hunger
back, and questions to the dark,
to fill yourself with seeds
black, verdant and reveled.

Persephone, I warned you
that you had to grow,
swallow seeded truth, bitter
melon. Take my gift to you,
the blame.

Kitchen Table

Give your sins,
the spilled coffee, forgotten wine.
Crown me with paper plates, pizza boxes
sweating through skin.
I remember in water stains,
beer bottle bottoms and soup rings.
I am covered.
The cat and the tablecloth,
gingham and lacquered wood,
sunning in your secrets.
They will never leave us.

Homecoming

In the space between us, empty
comfort pillows and wrinkled sheets.
Myself and the mattress,
breathless at the way you tuck your body
away. How can I share the space
of the green blanket, loved
long before you left yourself
soldier, casualty of sleep.

Lake Winfield

In the grey morning
reaching for my mother's hand
on the stale beach where I learned to swim,
we watched the geese refuse to leave,
clinging to silt, pressed
beneath fanned feet.
They belong to the sand,
and my mother tells me it is time
to go. Leaving me to the mud and geese,
she drops my hand and goes.

Mnemosyne

There's a song I chase
'round the corners of my head.
It sings,
whispers,
whoops
sweet and low in notes
I must have heard,
somewhere, sometime
I can't remember.

This Morning

I want to wake up in a bed with white covers
and the sun tickling our skin.
You would open your eyes half-way,
and let a smile steal your lips before I claim them.
We are warm
and I am safe under cotton sheets
and the strength of your arms.
You are a lion in the morning,
with heavy limbs and gentle words.
I think this as I touch your face,
as we breathe.
I crave
to wake up with you
always.

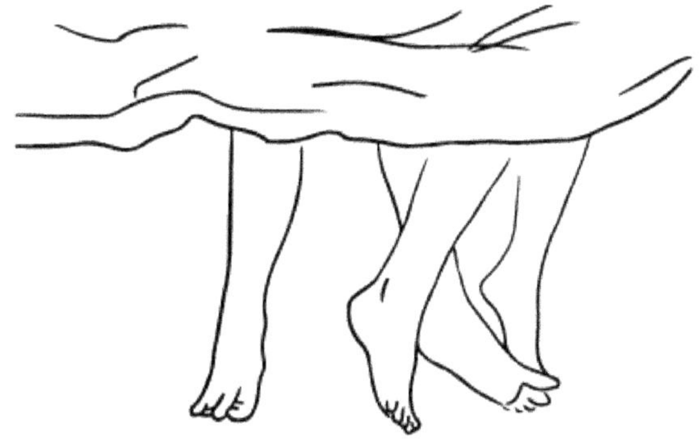